For my mother
CT

With very special thanks to Nghiem Ta

Text copyright © 2025 by Chi Thai
Illustrations copyright © 2025 by Dao Thuy Linh

First US edition 2025
First published by Walker Books Ltd. (UK) 2025

Library of Congress Catalog Card Number 2024944000
ISBN 978-1-5362-3960-7

24 25 26 27 28 29 APS 10 9 8 7 6 5 4 3 2 1

Printed in Humen, Dongguan, China

This book was typeset in Perpetua.
The illustrations were created digitally.

Candlewick Press
99 Dover Street
Somerville, Massachusetts 02144

www.candlewick.com

EU Authorized Representative: HackettFlynn Ltd.,
36 Cloch Choirneal, Balrothery, Co. Dublin, K32 C942, Ireland.
EU@walkerpublishinggroup.com

The ENDLESS SEA

CHI THAI

ILLUSTRATED BY

LINH DAO

CANDLEWICK PRESS

I was born after a long war ended.
I lived in a village, a tiger's whisker
away from the jungle.

It was my mother
and father
and sister
and me.
Together.

The war was over,
but life wasn't easier.
Everyone was hungry.
Everyone was afraid.

My family were punished for being
on the losing side of the war—
our relatives went missing.

Every day felt like it could be our last.

After New Year, Mum decided we had to leave.
She sold everything we had for gold.
She said this would pay for our new life.

She spoke to a man,
who spoke to another man,
who spoke to another man.
A deal was struck.

We waited until, at last, it was time to go.
We left at night so no one would see us.
If we were caught, we would be punished.

The crickets sang as we walked under the light of the moon.
When my legs grew tired, my mum carried me.

An old friend hid us in her home by the river.
If we were discovered, she would be punished too.
We could make no sound. We could leave no trace.

Finally we boarded a wooden boat.
We went deep into her belly.
Squeezed side by side, we couldn't
even wiggle our toes.

The boat's engine gurgled and spat.
Her smoke plumes rose as she
spluttered down the muddy river.

On the first day, we ate rice cakes.
On the second day, they were all gone.
On the third day, the water ran out.
On the fourth day, we reached the sea.
I shivered at the sight of it.
So big, so deep.

The night was studded with stars.
We sang to pass the time.
We sang because we could not sleep.

On the fifth day, heavy rains fell
and the boat's pump gave out.
We began to sink.

People climbed over each other
to reach the highest point.
My mother held me tightly.
I had never seen her so afraid.

Then, in the distance, a ship.
A speck at first—but it
came closer and closer,
growing bigger and bigger.

When the ship finally reached
us, I thought we were saved.
It was enormous.

But then an hour passed. Then another. And another.

Still the water rose.
What were they waiting for?
Our boat began to sink faster.

As the water inched higher and higher, I imagined
sinking with the boat and disappearing into the sea.
It would be as if we were never here, or never even existed.

Suddenly, ropes came down.
Mum was too weak to climb,
so sailors hoisted us
up on a pallet.

I looked back and caught one last glimpse of the boat
before it disappeared under the waves.

When my toes landed on the cold steel of the ship,
the storm I had been holding inside came raging out.
A storm of relief and joy and guilt. My tears poured and poured.

My mother scooped me up and held me close. Then, for the first
time in days, she smiled—and with her smile, my storm lifted.

The ship carried us to a new city,
where we stayed in a refugee camp—
until an airplane flew us to a new country . . .
and a bus took us to our new home.

WEEK ENDING JUNE 19, 1981

THE LUCKY ONES

B. WATSON MEETS A
RELIEVED BOAT FAMILY

WHEN their fragile boat started to fill
with water in the South China Sea, this

The family starve
as they hoped for
The horizon wa
shape of a ship
rescue was in

Some nights, I dream of that moment
when I was most afraid. I dream
that I'm falling through the water . . .
deeper and deeper, until I reach
those who weren't so lucky.
There are so many of us.

We are all falling:
deeper and deeper,
into the endless sea.

But we are the lucky ones.
We are safe.

I live in a small town now.
My school is a cat's whisker
away from my new home.

New Year is here again.
We eat until we are no longer hungry
and sing songs about days yet to come.

Days with my mother
and father
and sister
and me.
Together.

AUTHOR'S NOTE

I was three years old when I left my birth country, Vietnam, and came to the UK as a refugee.

After the long war ended in Vietnam, there was a new government that targeted people from the South—who were on the losing side. My family, like many others, were forced to surrender our home and burn our belongings. Leaving became the only means of survival.

My mother traded all we had left for passage on a boat—praying we could overcome the dangerous seas and reach a safe future. We did not know where that would be.

Our boat, like so many of the wooden boats that the Vietnamese used to escape, was made poorly and quickly. It did not take long or much for these boats to fail, and it is estimated that between 200,000 and 400,000 died at sea.

But my family and I were lucky. We survived.

My story is one of many. And this is not my whole story, by any stretch: our escape and rescue were, in fact, only the beginning of our journey. What happened next is another story.

When I made that journey, there were over 6 million refugees around the world. Today, there are more than 110 million people forcibly displaced, with over 36 million refugees. Now, more than ever, it's vital to understand the profound challenges faced by those forced to flee. The need for our compassion is urgent.

Chi Thai